# NEEDLE FELTING FOR BEGINNERS

## A BEGINNER'S GUIDE

Copyright@2022

Grace Stacey

# Table of Content

# CHAPTER ONE

## NEEDLE FELTING

Needle Felting is the process of changing wool into three-dimensional objects with a barbed needle. When wool is felted, the fibers are agitated until they bind together, creating a solid cloth. Needle felting, a form of art that utilizes traditional felting processes, is a fun and fascinating hobby that enables you to make gorgeous felted sculptures, paintings, and decorations. Using a felting needle to poke wool compresses the fibers to make felt.

Needle felting, also known as dry felting, is a craft that is gaining popularity rapidly due to the vast number of creative options it offers. Participation is relatively easy to attain. With some wool fibers (or a non-wool substitute) and a designed especially felting needle with small rungs that grab and entangle the fibers once inserted, it is possible to create nearly any three-dimensional shape. As the needle is repeatedly plugged and eliminated, the wool fibers shrink and become firmer over time, allowing the artisan to sculpt the wool into the desired form. Wool as a form of media has the possibilities to closely resemble animal fur; consequently, needle felting is becoming the technique of choice for many artists who wish to create lifelike animal sculptures, ranging from common cats and dogs to a vast array of unusual creatures. Equally, the vibrant array of colors available in felting wool and fibers lend themselves to the creation of jewelry, charms, home decor, paintings, wall art, and much more.

SUPPLIES NEEDED

1. A block of foam with open cells

2. A maximum of two needle felting needles. (A bigger and a smaller is fantastic.)

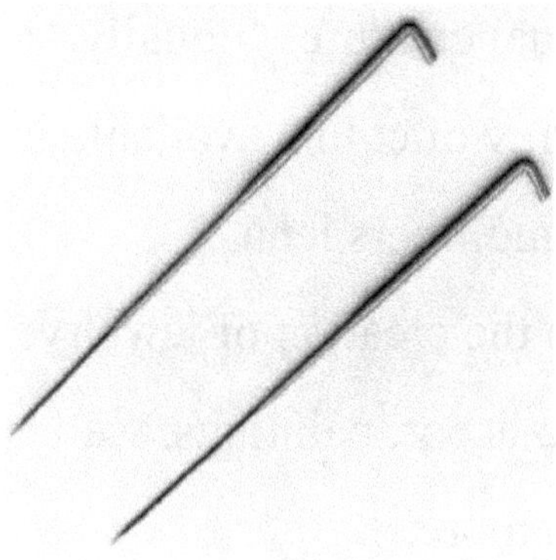

3. Unspun wool that is clean.

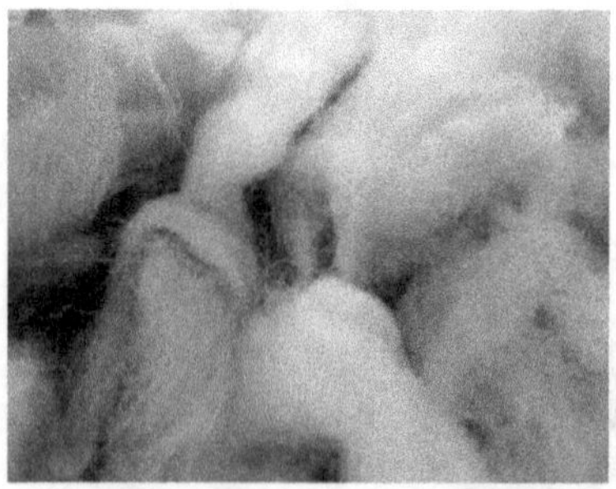

4. Safety gear (a couple of thimbles or something to protect your fingers from wayward strikes.)

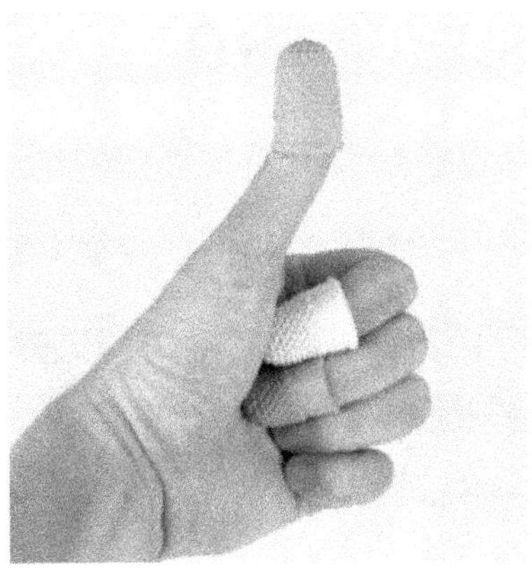

5. Lastly, your shape will require a background or form.

# CHAPTER TWO

## PROJECTS ON NEEDLE FELTING

## PROJECT ONE- WHAT TO DO TO CREATE A FELTED WOOL STAR THROUGH NEEDLE FELTING

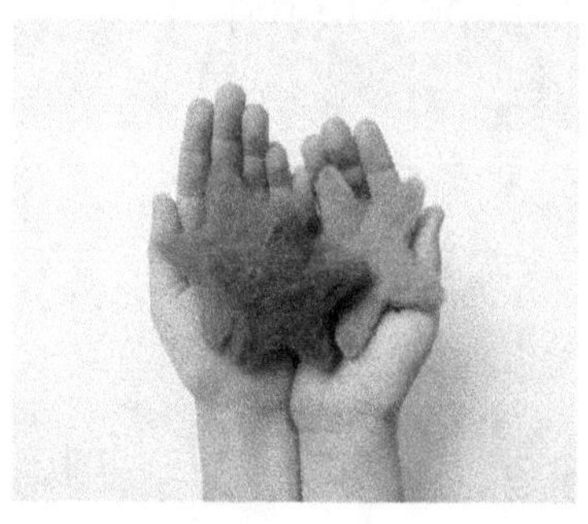

## Materials

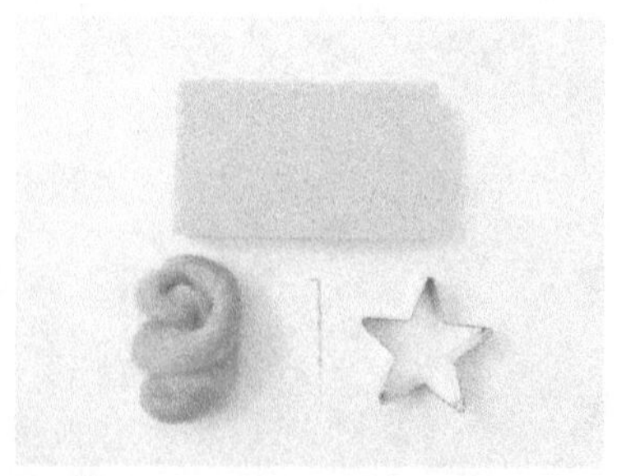

- Sheep's wool

- Fiber needle

- Abundant sponge

- Cookie Cutter

Step 1

From the bigger piece of roving, gently separate short "drafts" or pieces of wool.

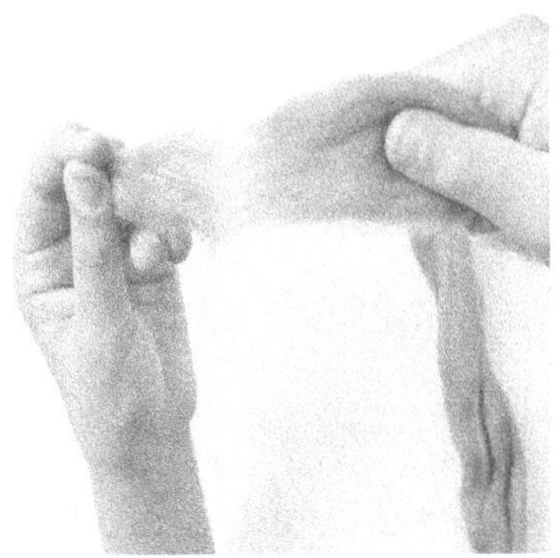

Step 2

Begin with the cookie cutter on the sponge and fill the inside of the cookie cutter with the just-drawn sketches. Attempt to maintain a consistent level of wool throughout the form, and fill it to the brim with the material.

Step 3

Start poking the wool with your felting needle. Concentrate on the star's edges and corners and strive for consistency in your work.

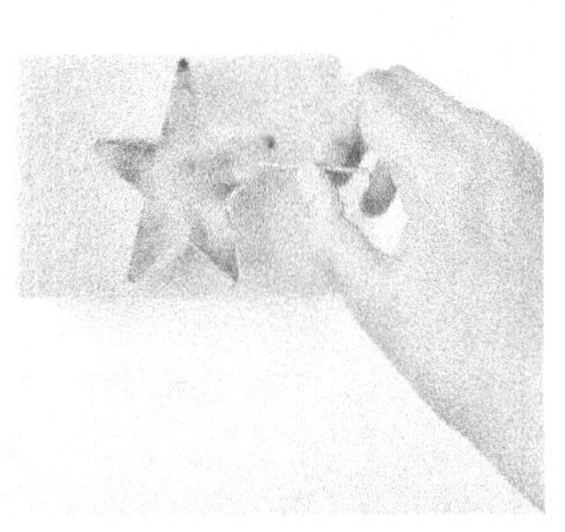

Step 4

After one to two minutes of prodding the wool with the felting needle, the wool will be felted into the desired shape.

Step 5

To prevent your item from clinging
too much to the sponge, you must
pick up the cookie cutter and the wool
and flip them over. Continue piercing
the wool with the felting needle for
one to two minutes on this side.
Repeat steps 3–5, turning the project
over and felting the wool until the
wool becomes dense and retains its
shape.

Step 6

Remove the cookie cutter once the
wool has felted sufficiently to retain
its shape.

Step 7

Use the felting needle to continue
refining the shape. Focus on the edges
with special care. If there is a bump or
an uneven edge, repeatedly insert the
needle into it. The wool will then feel,
and the lump will diminish.

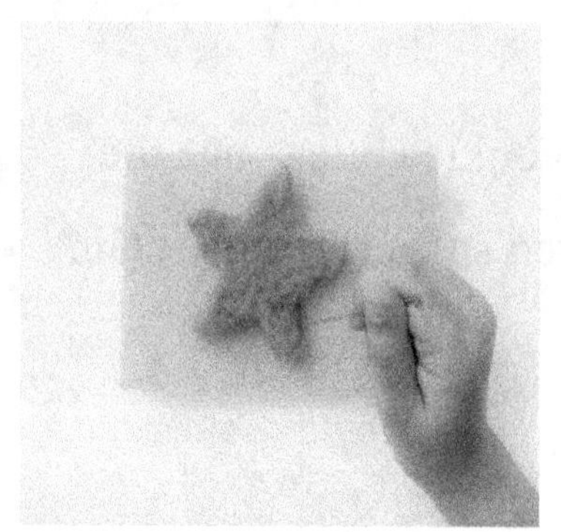

# PROJECT 2- HOW TO NEEDLE-FELT A CUTE PUMPKIN

1. We will begin by creating an orange ball for the pumpkin. Remove a length of orange wool roving roughly the size of your hand and roll it between your palms.

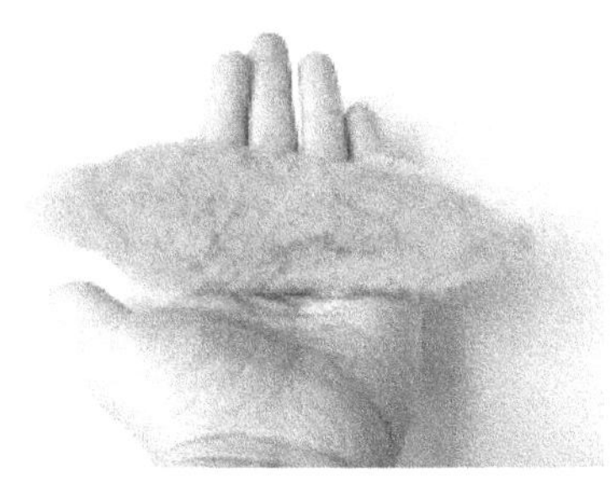

2. Create a tight, thick spiral with the wool "snake." The fitted it can be pulled, the simpler it will be to felt. The thicker your spiral, the rounder your ball will be.

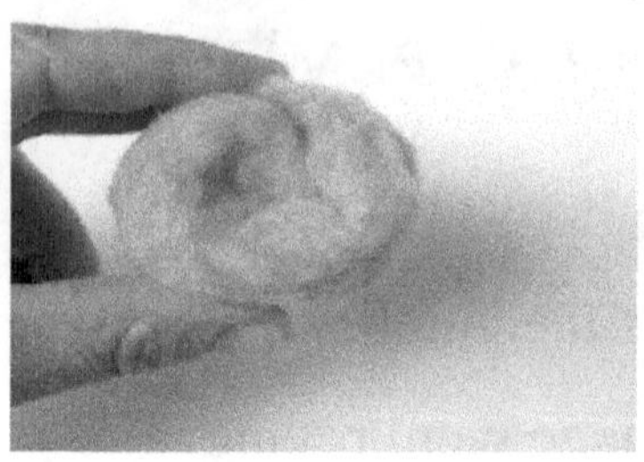

3. Once the orange wool has already been coiled together into tight, fat spiral, place it on the felting board and pierce it with the needle several times around the exterior of the spiral. Be deliberate and slow with your initial thrusts, and please maintain focus.

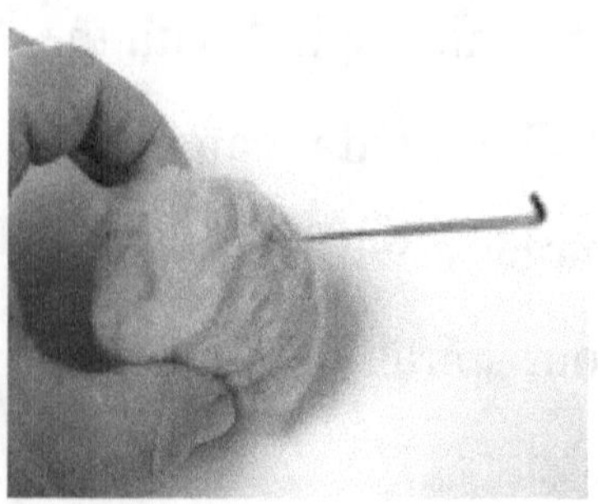

4. Next, to tidy up the surface of the orange ball and make it spherical, use your thumb and index finger to gently pull the outer layer of wool a bit looser. Fold this layer over the spiraled wool and gently needle feel it. Repeat with the opposite' spiral' end of your ball and needle felt it until it is a smooth round ball.

5. Using a needle and thread, we will create the "segments" of your pumpkin. Thread the needle using a

color-coordinated, robust thread. Use thread for needlework. Make a knot at the end of the thread and use a basic catch stitch to 'catch' the thread in the pumpkin's base (through a little roving at the base of your pumpkin, and through again, catching the roving in the stitch firmly). Then, while placing your 'pumpkin ball' horizontally, run the needle through the ball from the bottom of the pumpkin to the top middle, where the stalk will go.

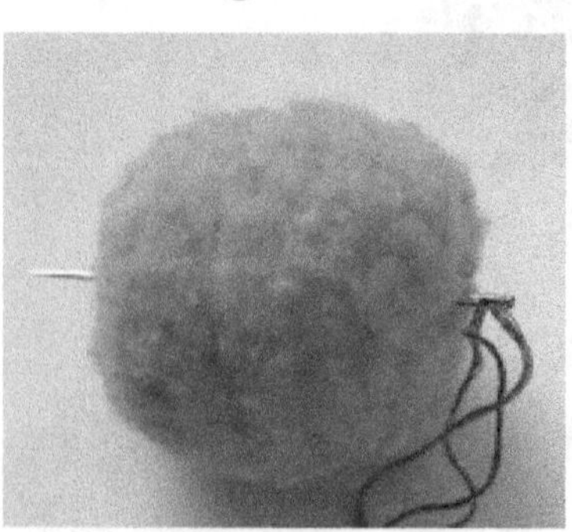

6. Pinch the pumpkin ball securely between your thumb and forefinger, then tighten the thread by pulling it taut. Pass the thread over the exterior of the ball and then through it again, as described previously, while maintaining a firm grip on the ball with your thumb and forefinger. Pull firmly, and you will notice that the thread on the exterior of the pumpkin ball will create a perfect pumpkin indentation around the ball's exterior. Still pinching the ball between your thumb and forefinger and spacing the next thread segment a little distance apart from the first thread segment, repeat, passing the thread around the outside of the ball again and back

through the center, tightening when it emerges at the stalk end of the pumpkin ball. You will notice that you've created a flawless pumpkin segment.

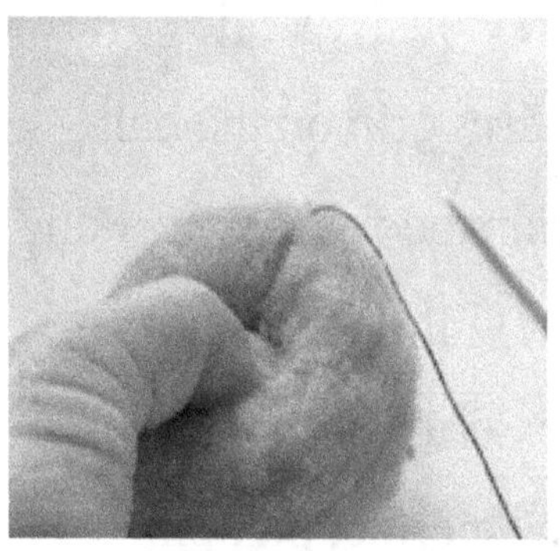

7. Keep making string sections all the way around the pumpkin ball, ensuring that the distance between each segment is nearly the same.

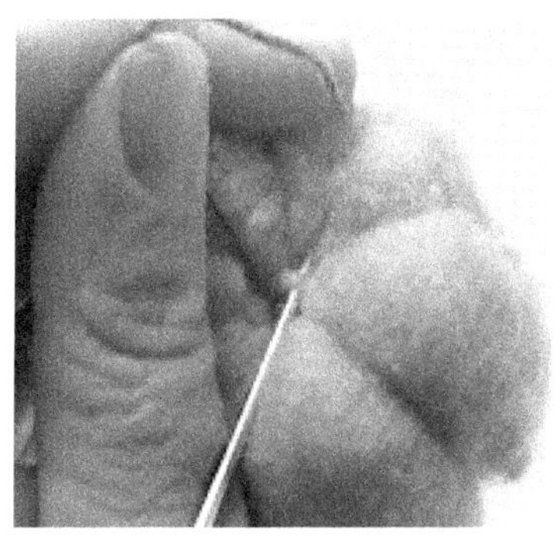

8. Once all of your segments are finished, you can either tie a knot in the thread, again using a simple catch stitch in the wool at the base of the pumpkin, or clip the thread. Alternatively, if you choose to hang your pumpkin, feed the thread back through the middle of the pumpkin after creating the catch thread. Create a loop for hanging, then feed the thread back through the pumpkin's middle. Cut short the thread.

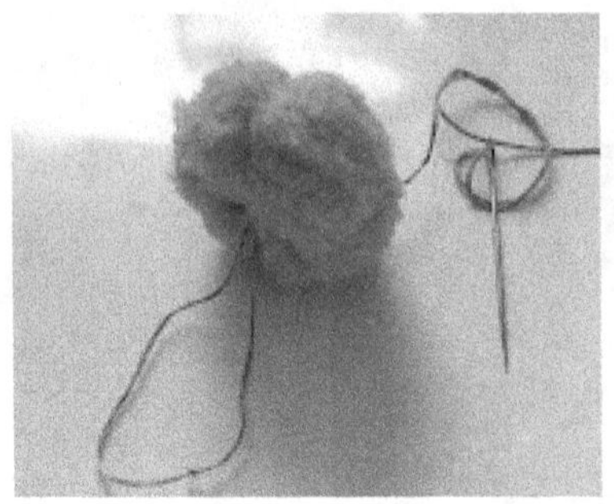

9. All of this manipulation of your orange pumpkin ball has likely rendered it extremely fuzzy. Using a felting needle, restore the fuzz and pay close attention to the segment indentations of the pumpkin. Ensuring that they have beautiful, straight lines.

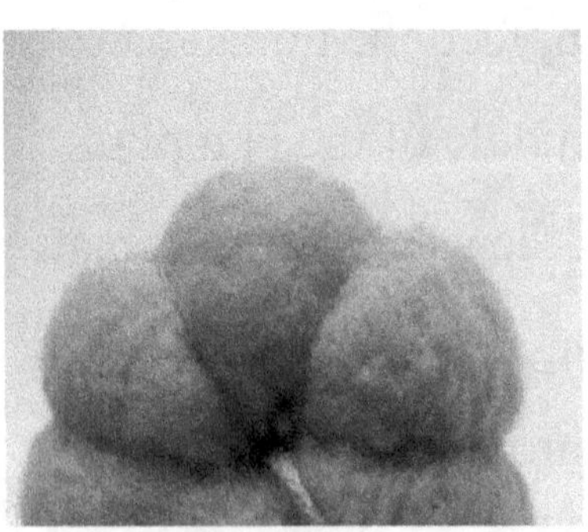

10. Create the green stem leaf and twisting vine at this time. Make a tiny piece of green wool around half an inch long and the size of your little finger. As you would with a ball of playdough, shape it with your hands into a snake.

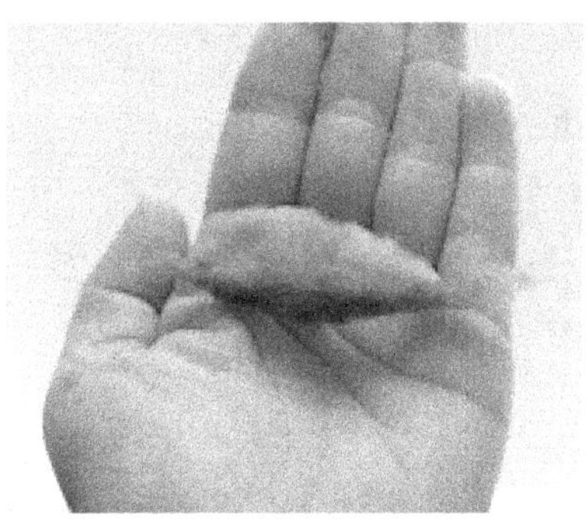

11. Turn this "snake" into a tight, little spiral. While still securely clutching the little green spiral, place it on the felting board and needle felt along the spiral's outside edge. Let one end

hang loose. Carefully felt the opposite end with a needle.

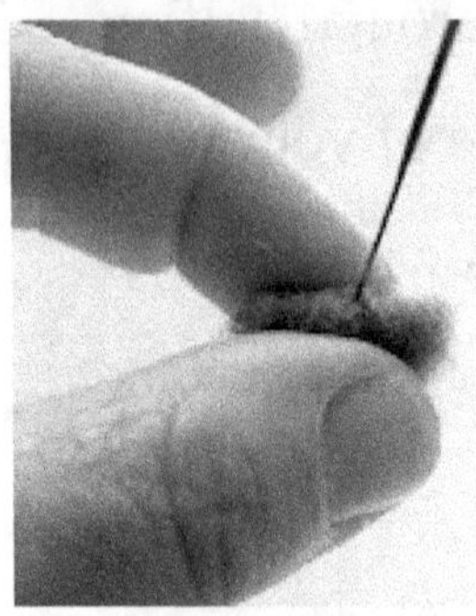

12. Now, attach the stem to the pumpkin and needle-felt the fluffy end into the orange, indented tip of the pumpkin, attempting to conceal the thread used to make the segmented design. Stitch it onto your orange pumpkin with a needle.

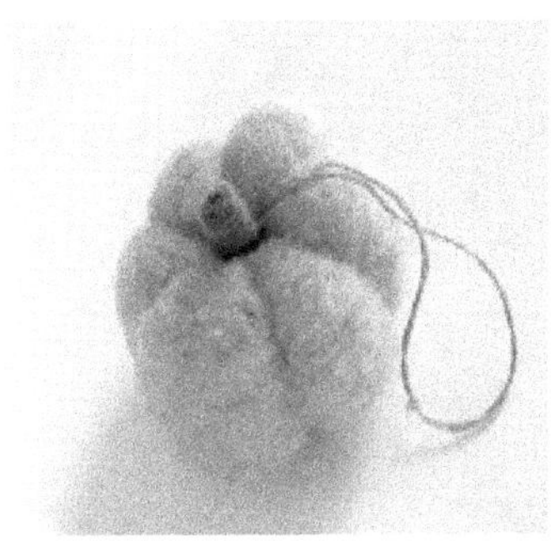

13. To create the twirl vine, take an even smaller piece of green wool and roll it between your palms, tugging it in the direction of the long axis, until you get a thread-like length. It can be needle felted onto the pumpkin.

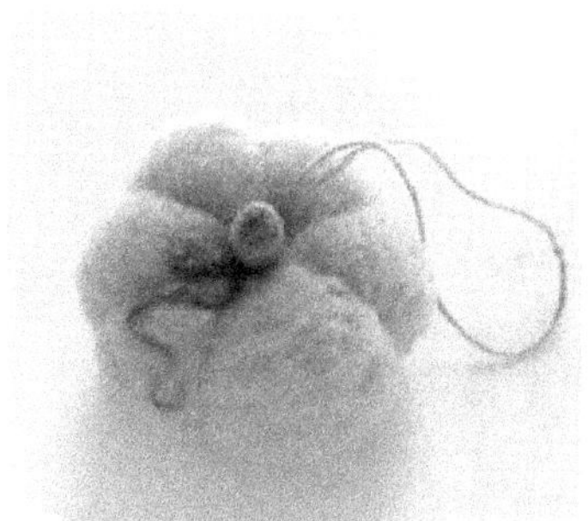

# PROJECT 3- HOW TO MAKE EASTER EGGS WITH NEEDLE FELTING

## Materials:

- Styrofoam egg form or Felt Egg Blank

- wool roving in the colors of your choice (only small amount required)

- Med/Fine Felting needle

- Foam pad

**INSTRUCTIONS**

1. Cover your Styrofoam egg with several thin layers of wool roving to begin.

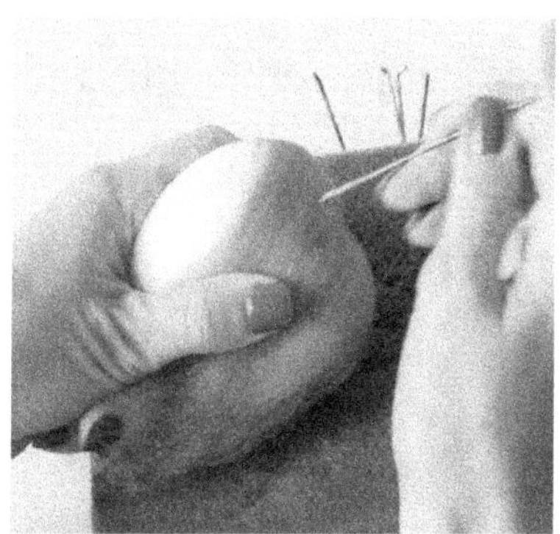

2. Place little bits of wool roving on the egg's surface and puncture them with a felting needle as you go.

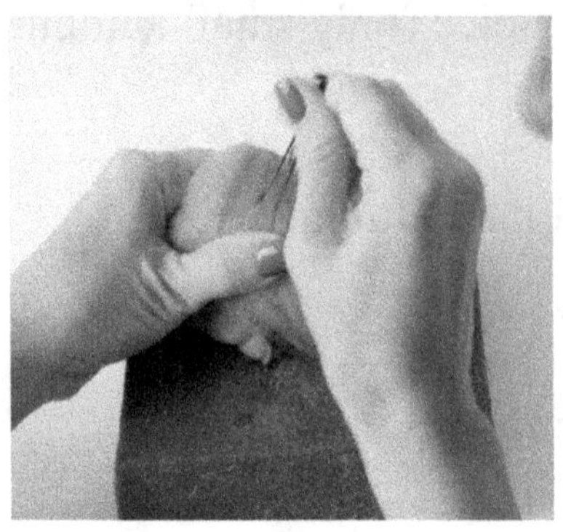

3. Continue needling the entire surface of the egg form to secure and smooth the roving. The more you prod the surface with your needle, the smoother it will become. Continue to add little, fluffed bits of roving to cover any bare spots.

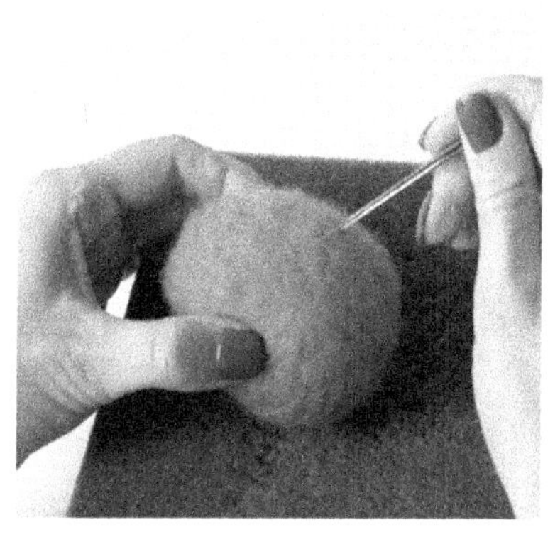

4. Once you are satisfied with the coverage and density of the wool layer, you may begin decorating your felted Easter egg.

5. Be inventive when designing your surface. If you are new to needle felting, Spots is the easiest pattern to start with.

6. To create spots, roll a small bit of wool between your fingers to form a small ball.

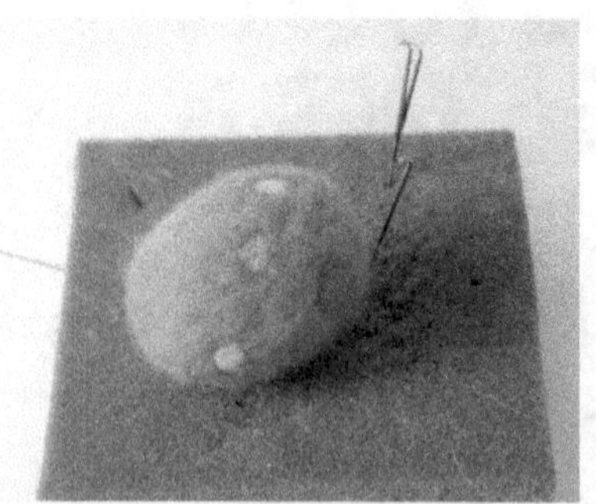

7. Stretch the small ball of roving between your fingers and insert it in the desired location. Stick it with the felting needle until it adheres to the bottom layer.

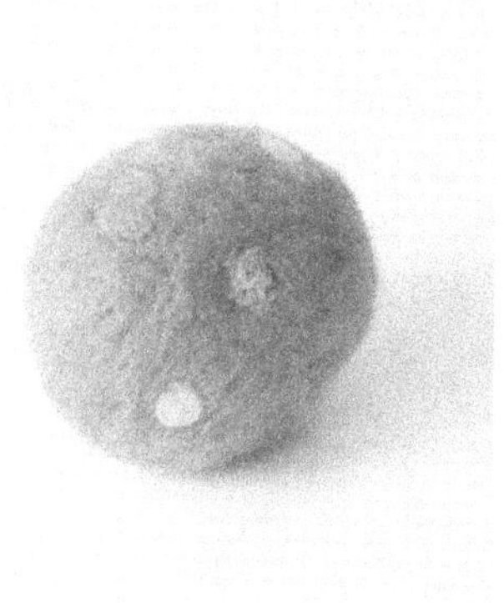

8. Continue to add spots until you are satisfied with the design. To complete the pattern, give the egg's surface a last needling to smooth it out.

# PROJECT 4- NEEDLE FELTING TO REPAIR WOOL HOLES

Step 1: Insert little chunks of roving directly through the hole to ensure it is plugged, then begin stabbing. Continue to add roving and hold it up to the light to ensure that no light can pass through.

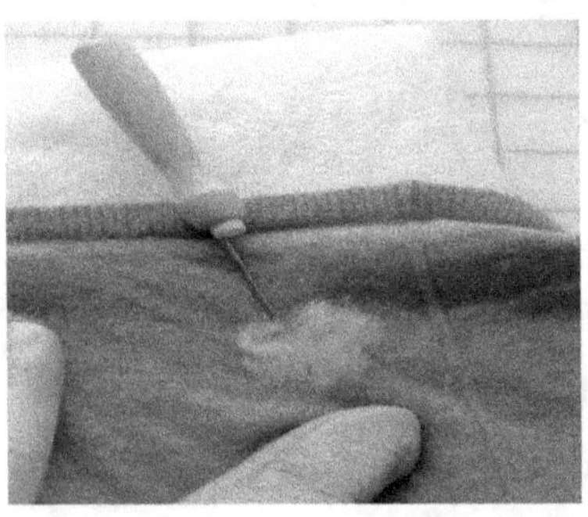

Step 2: Flip it inside out and, if necessary, apply more roving to this side until it feels even.

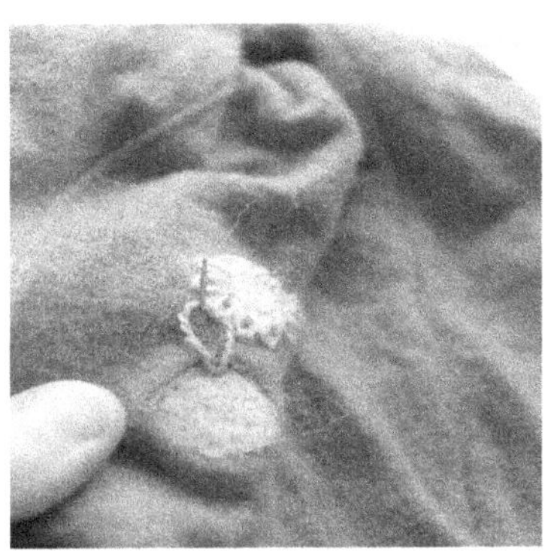

Step 3: Begin the lazy daisy stitch.
Knot the end of your floss; come up
and down in the same hole, but don't
pull too tightly; leave a loop hanging.

Step 4: Carefully emerge under the
bottom of your knot and afterwards

back in over the top to create a small
anchoring point.

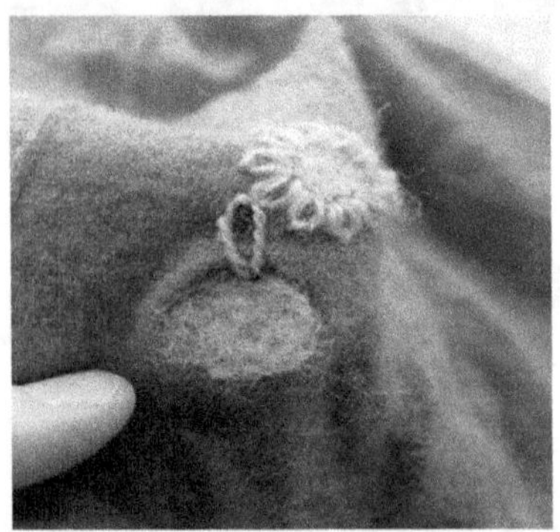

Repetition encircling the center! This
is how a single petal will appear.